Cats WHO Quilt

The First Quilting Book for Cats!

Written by Judy Heim

Illustrated by Irina Borisova

FRUITFUL PLAINS
Madison, Wisconsin

We lovingly dedicate this book to our mothers Esther and Asya.

Fruitful Plains
Post Office Box 5056
Madison, Wisconsin 53705

Library of Congress Cataloging-in-Publication Data
Heim, Judy.
   Cats who quilt: the first quilting book for cats /
Judy Heim and Irina Borisova
         p.   cm.
   ISBN 0-9700936-0-8 (Paper trade)
   1. Cats-Humor. 2. Quilting-Humor. 3. Art-Humor.
     I. Title
Library of Congress Control Number: 2001118738

Design Director/Book Designer: Christina D. Jarumay
Production Manager: Christina D. Jarumay
Cover Illustration: Irina Borisova
Cover Design: Irina Borisova and Christina D. Jarumay
Editor: Harry McCracken
A special thanks to Joni Prittie and her cat
for inspirations.

Printed in China.
10 9 8 7 6 5 4 3 2 1

SUPERVISE THOSE CATS WHO QUILT!

This book arose in response to the popularity of The Cat Quilt Web Site (**http://www.catswhoquilt.com**). For the past five years, quilters have written to me with stories about the cats who follow them devotedly around their sewing room or perch on their lap as they stitch. Quilters have also shared sad stories about cats who have died after ingesting thread or other sewing notions.

Cats love sewing baskets. A spool of thread is a marvelous toy to bat across the floor. But please keep an eye on your cat as she's playing in your sewing room. Cats, like children, will swallow nearly anything they can get into their mouths. So will dogs.

If you spot your cat swallowing thread do not pull it out of the cat's mouth. The thread may have worked its way into the cat's stomach. Take your pet immediately to an animal hospital and ask a veterinarian to remove the thread.

Here are important tips for keeping your pets safe in your sewing room:

■ Store Needles Carefully, Especially When Threaded

Elaine on AOL writes: "Ever since I found one of my cats with 12 inches of thread down her throat, and the needle wedged in her mouth, I keep needles unthreaded when I'm not using them. My cat did not need expensive veterinary treatment, but my vet told me that swallowing threaded needles is a common life-threatening accident for cats."

Elaine recommends storing threaded needles in a dome threaded needle case or "quilt dome." You can find these at most quilting stores.

■ Hide Thread, Especially From Kittens

"You must make your sewing room kitten-proof!" writes Dellie Morse. After Dellie found that her kitten had batted around a spool of thread, wrapping thread around chairs and table legs, she pulled a long

thread from his mouth. The next morning, when he began vomitting, she rushed him to the vet. The vet found thread wound around the cat's tongue, with both ends in his belly. He operated, and luckily Dellie's cat survived.

But the vet bill was over $1,000. (That's what many quilters report that they end up spending to save cats who have swallowed thread.) Dellie says she nows puts away every scrap of thread, as well as needles and pins, whenever she leaves her sewing machine.

■ Store Buttons, Pins, and Other Notions in Jars

One quilter wrote "I have 11 cats and they feel they are the masters of my sewing room. I am concerned about pins, needles, and thread. I have found that plastic and glass jars are easy to use to keep everything away from my animal companions. I store all my threads in gallon-sized glass jars with caps. I keep pins in a magnetic holder which fits, along with my scissors, into a wide-mouthed peanut butter jar."

■ Dispose of Plastic Bags

Jean Rabe in Vermont says she nearly lost her beloved cat to an intestinal blockage of thread and plastic. Many cats—as well as dogs—chew plastic bags, for animal fat is often used in the plastic's processing. Plastic can jam in a pet's intestines, and remain invisible to x-rays. Jean's cat survived, but "he still attacks my sewing machines/serger, biting the thread," she says, "so I cover them up with towels, and we never leave groceries in plastic bags."

■ Watch Out for Dogs, Too

Jean Fletcher writes that dogs like to paw through garbage cans, including those in sewing rooms. Quilters should keep trash cans far from inquisitive paws.

Please, please keep needles, pins, thread, and other notions away from pets!

PreFace
Supervise Those Cats Who Quilt!

Introduction
Clancy the Cat Explains Why He Decided
to Write a Quilting Book for Cats

Chapter 1

How to Get Started Quilting if You're a Cat

Quilting Lessons for Cats:

The Laws of Cat Quilting

CHAPTER II

A Gallery of Cat Quilts

CHAPTER V

CHAPTER VI

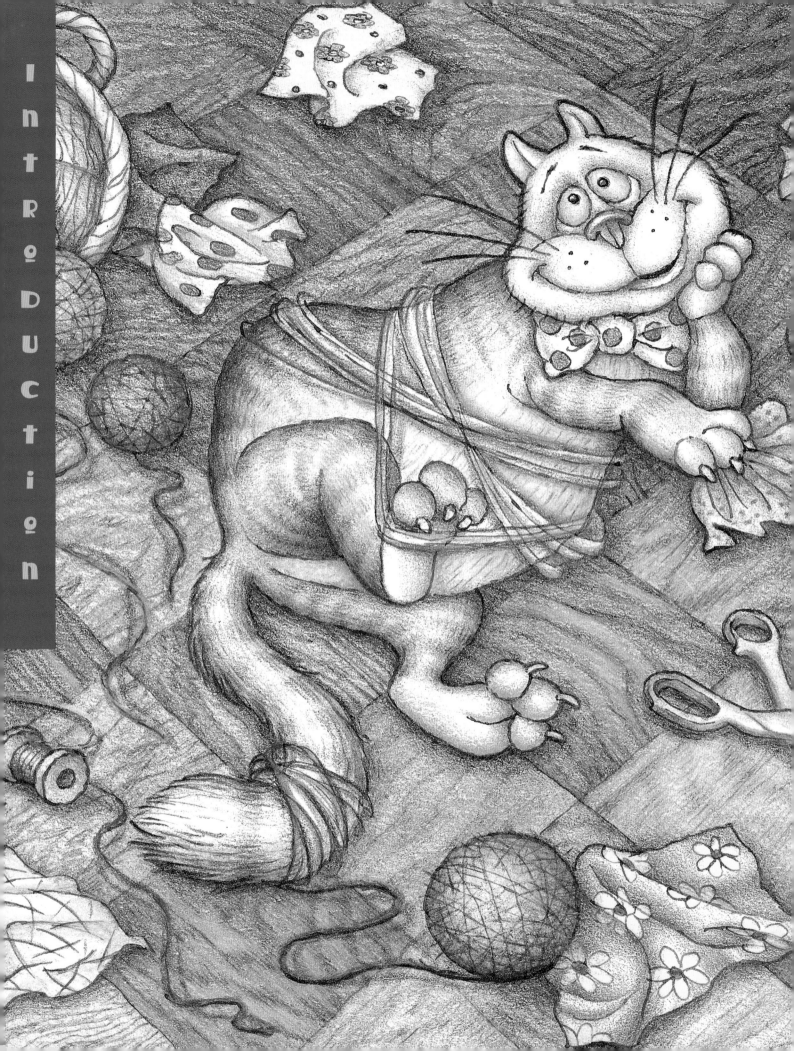

Clancy the Cat Explains Why He Decided to Write a Quilting Book for Cats

Hello, my name is Clancy du Cotton. I'm a big marmalade cat. I'm also a quilter. My artistic vision is bold. I leap on to quilting frames. I scurry under ironing boards. I roll across fabric spread across the floor, and chase quilt patches around the room as if they were butterflies.

When I am not quilting, I enjoy working in my sewing basket. I start by poking a paw into the basket when no one is looking. I grope until I feel something tangle around my claws. I roll onto my back and pull everything out of the basket. I bite thread, gnaw pincushions, and kick needle packets with my back feet. I smack and thrash until I'm wrapped in a rat's nest of thread and buttons. Hissing, I roll across the floor until I feel dizzy.

Regrettably, my euphoria is usually brief. As soon as my human quilting pal spots me, she runs into the room. "Clancy!" she cries, gasping. She nabs me, untangles the elastic thread from around my tummy, and pulls the fabric scraps from my paws. Then she clenches me to her chest. "Oh Clancy," she'll coo, smoothing my fur and kissing me. "I'm so glad you're not hurt!"

I also enjoy lap quilting. The combination of a warm lap to nest in and moving thread to swing paws at provides a contentment found nowhere else in the art world except by sitting by a gopher hole waiting for something to emerge.

But my favorite quilting technique is to simply follow my human quilting pal around as she bastes her quilt, pins quilt blocks together, and pulls fabric off the shelf. I mew encouragements, I rub against her legs, I step on fabric to help her choose colors. I flutter my tail to express my artistic opinions and make sure that no mice, raccoons, or voles run across the room.

When she tires, I encourage her to nap, preferably with me and preferably on the quilt on which we are working. When she fixes herself a snack, I remind her, by mewing and pacing, that cat treats are excellent nutritional supplements for a quilter.

I know there are many other cats who enjoy quilting as I do. What cat doesn't love the feel of calico scrunching beneath his toes as he scurries over it? What cat doesn't creep forward in fascination at the sight of thread being jerked in and out of fabric? What cat doesn't swing paws with excitement as the thread tangles?

Many cats love floral appliqué. When you're a cat, there is nothing like the thrill of turning a placid needle-turned bouquet into a hodgepodge of cotton leaves and petals that flutter as you hop over your human pal's lap and send everything she is struggling to stitch cascading to the floor.

Some cats find inspiration in ironing boards. They find that by sitting on one and peering over its edge to bat at the ironing board cover's strings, they can conjure memories of a vivid primordial past as a jungle cat perched atop a mountain surveying the colorful landscape.

Many cats' favorite quilting technique is strip piecing, which is also many humans' favorite way to assemble a quilt. They start by chewing one end of a strip of fabric. Then they chew more if it. They keep chewing until someone spots them and cries "Gimme that!" then snatches the cat and pulls the gooey fabric out of his spitting mouth.

Like the human quilt world, the cat quilt world is not without its controversies. One radical clowder of tabbies, for example, is bent upon turning the sedate art of quilt-making into boisterous political statements with their performance art. These felines attack paper templates with claws, knock plastic stencils under rugs, and turn fabric into cat origami. When their distraught humans remove them to a far corner of the house so that they may resume their quilt-making in peace, the exiled cats howl at the social injustice of it all.

Despite all this activity by cats in sewing rooms around the world, there have been until now no quilting books for cats. I hope to remedy that tragedy with this humble manual. I want other cats to discover the joys of disrupting craft projects, falling off sewing machines, and burrowing into piles of sewing projects for a nap. I want other cats to know that even though they are dangerous carnivores, there is no shame in spending an afternoon knocking thread bobbins off a sewing machine and watching them hit the floor with an amusing ker-plunk! I want other animals to know that there are other emotionally gratifying ways of spending an evening besides sitting atop a warm TV.

It is my hope that you, my dear feline friend, you will learn how to determine which quilts in your house are the softest to nest in, which pieces of sewing room furniture will be the most fun to hop on and knock over with a clatter, and, most importantly, how to help your human friend sew quilts that are true to her artistic vision, as well as that of her quilting cat.

Clancy du Cotton
Pawducah, Kentucky

How to Get Started Quilting if You're a Cat

"I haven't actually seen my cat Brandy quilting, but sometimes I find my rotary blades duller than I left them, and once, when I got up in the middle of the night, I found the Singer Featherweight warm. I haven't found any of her quilts--she's either sending them to homeless kitties or they are unfinished-objects hidden in the closet."

— BECKY WALL,
WILMINGTON, DELAWARE

Start your quilting session by jumping on top the ironing board.
Sit very still and pretend. Pretend that you are a jungle cat perched
on a high precipice and gazing out over the plains. Pretend that
you are a lion preparing to leap atop a sewing machine.

Quilting Lessons For Cats

We cats are born quilters. That's because we spend most of our lives sleeping. Who better to create a quilt than the creature who most hopes to sleep on it? If you have never quilted before, this chapter will show you the first steps, like how to sit on an ironing board and how to procure a sewing basket for yourself. Do not worry if you cannot fit a thimble on any of your claws. And don't fret if you cannot curl your entire body inside your mistress's sewing basket. As a cat quilter, all you'll need to know about most sewing notions is how to smack them off a sewing table and watch them roll under the couch.

Lesson #1 What to Do With an Ironing Board

If you are a cat who is new to quilting, the first piece of sewing room equipment that you will find yourself drawn to is the ironing board. Like a catwalk stretching over a sea of dropped pins and fabric, the ironing board rises magnificently from a corner of the sewing room, beckoning you to jump on it. While humans might argue that these padded catwalk wannabees were created for ironing things flat, we cats know that they

were actually designed for sitting atop and daydreaming. More specifically, they were invented for perching on and pretending that one is a panther crouched on a high precipice and gazing out over the plains.

This is a perfect way to begin a quilting session. Jump on the ironing board, sit very still, and pretend. Pretend that you are a lion about to rush through the jungle and leap atop a sewing machine. Pretend that you are a cougar preparing to bare your powerful claws and pull a spool of thread from a sewing basket. Pretend that you are a leopard about to roar and knock scissors on the floor. Each of these moves must be considered carefully, for artists are careful creatures.

Whatever you do as you daydream, do not tip the ironing board over. Panthers never tip over their mountain precipices. Nor should you let your tail flip too near the hot iron perched on the board. If it does, the iron might scorch it. And what will happen then? Your human will scoop you up and rush you to a vet who will soothe your tender tail and may send you home with a pink bow tied around your neck. And everyone knows that pink bows do not flatter fearsome panthers, even those who quilt.

Lesson #2 Finding and Using a Sewing Basket

Once you find a sewing basket and learn to use it effectively, you will wonder how it is possible that our ancestors stalked the African plains for generations without them.

Every cat needs a sewing basket. Reaching into one is like pawing through a treasure chest heaped with cat toys. You will probably find a sewing basket sitting near your human as she stitches her quilt or irons. Approach it quietly, so she doesn't hear you.

Ideally, the basket will be open. If it's not, you can easily flick its top off with a paw. That done, reach in and feel around. Grope until you feel something snag around your claws. This should not take long. There are many things in the basket that, when teased, will tangle around your paw: snarls of thread, unwound cards of seam binding, bits of lace. Even a snip of paper bearing a hand-written poem will, when properly provoked, impale itself on your claws.

When your paw feels heavy from all the objects tangled around it, flip onto your back and pull everything out of the basket. Bite pincushions. Snap thread with your teeth. Toss spools in the air. Kick them with your back feet. Your goal should that of a juggler: to propel as many objects as high into the air as possible and bounce them off your paws. That accomplished, roll across the floor.

When your human rushes to unwind the rick-rack from around your ears and loosen the ribbon from your paws, mew sadly, as if none of this was your fault. Then hop to your feet, turn, and scamper off so that the contents of the basket trail you like baubles from a king's upended play chest.

There are many things in sewing baskets that, when properly teased, will tangle around your feet and paws. Even a snip of paper bearing a hand-written poem will, when properly provoked, impale itself on your claws.

Lesson #3 How to Supervise a Human Quilter

Humans need plenty of supervision when they quilt. They may stitch long and duteously, but in their industry they often forget to stop and play. You need to remind them by reaching up from their lap to bat at their earrings, or by tunneling under the fabric jumbled on their knees, or by knocking their thimbles onto the floor.

Human quilters also get lonely as they sew. Some quilters talk to their cats as they stitch, spilling out their woes. If this sounds like your human, you should pretend to listen. But remember that as a supervisor you don't want to get too emotionally involved. When your human despairs of insensitive spouses who grouse when their bare toes impale themselves on sewing pins, stare at her, eyes wide, interested, but aloof. When she prattles about the high cost of jungle-print fabric, flip your tail with concern. You may occasionally bow your head in thought, but don't let on that you actually care.

The best way to supervise is curled in a lap. This way your human can scratch your ears between stitches or scissors snips. As she sews, you should watch her hands carefully, occasionally rubbing your cheek against them to elicit caresses. Should a strand of thread wiggle from her hands, don't hesitate to bat at it. That's part of your job as supervisor. Be warned that if your human is hunched over a quilting frame, you may occasionally bump your head on the frame when you peek up to see how she is progressing.

The next best place to supervise is crunched on a couch arm. You can keep an eye on the fabric heaped on the floor in case any rodents run out from under it. You'll also be the first to know when your human gets up to get a snack, and can quickly fly to her heels.

You should stay clear of sewing machines, though. Their cabinets often bounce and their motors groan as they stitch, two nasty habits that disqualify them as cat beds.

Finally, a good spot from which to supervise is seated on a half-basted quilt that's stretched on the floor. Find the softest part of the quilt, prance toward it and claim it as your throne. Sit still as a gargoyle and stare like one, your tail curled around you. Your human, when faced with such a willful stare, will have no choice but to hurry to finish her quilt so that she can arrange it on a bed for you, her beloved friend, to sleep on.

Lesson #4 How to Calculate Fabric Yardage if You're a Cat

When human quilters start assembling a quilt they like to figure out how much fabric they'll need to buy. They devote much time to twiddling with a pencil, paper, and yardstick, measuring patches, calculating sizes, even stretching a tape measure the length of a bed. As a cat quilter you have a more efficient method: You merely need to know how much fabric you must have to knead a soft pile into which you may curl to take a nap. The ideal amount: 30 to 150 yards.

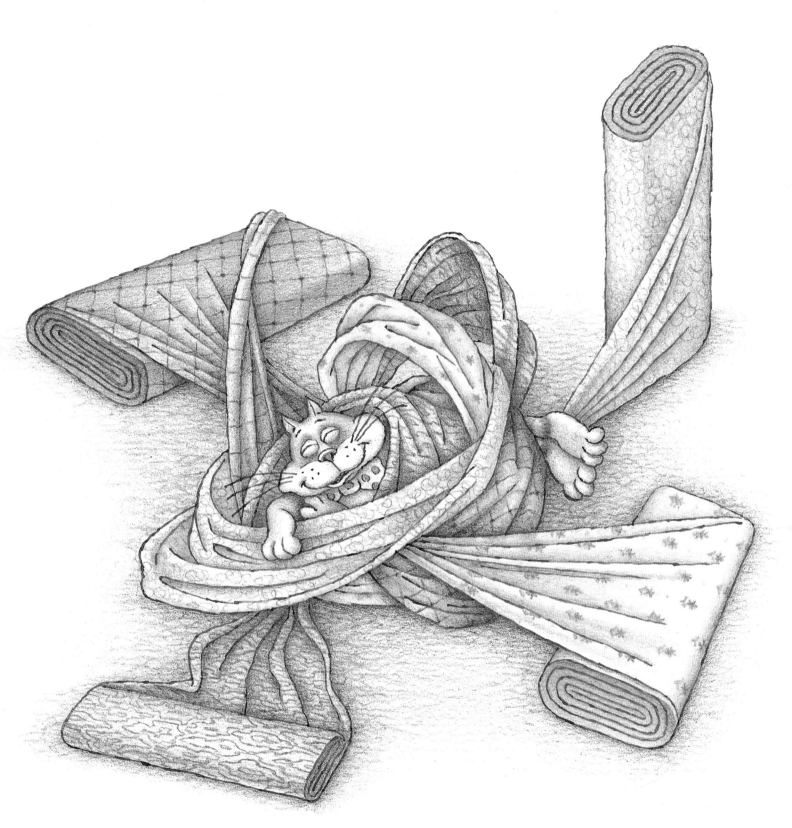

As a cat quilter you need to determine how much fabric you must have in order to knead a soft pile into which you may curl to take a nap.

Lesson #5 How to Arrange Quilt Patches With Your Toes

The scenario is this: Your human has arranged the pieces of her half-stitched quilt top on the floor. She is either fussily sewing and pinning it, or else she is standing back to apprise her carefully arranged blocks and patches. As you saunter into the room, your thoughts will fly to all the different ways you can make her feeble efforts look better.

Before you race across the quilt and send its scraps flying into a more charming arrangement, stop to consider your options. You don't want to let on that you don't think your human's handiwork is very good. On the other hand, the quilt top must be rearranged quickly, while there's still time to save it. You have no time for diplomacy. What's more, you need to be out of the room by the time the quilt patches stop fluttering. Here are strategies for prettying up your human's ho-hum quilt:

Act Like You Have Someplace to Go, and the Quilt Is in Your Way. This should not be hard. As a cat you always have someplace to go. As you galumph over the quilt, keep your head high and flex your claws so that they snag loose fabric patches and drag them along. Should your human stretch her arms out to remove you, flash her that haughty glare that causes her to freeze in intimidation. Keep prancing.

Should she cry "No, no! Get off that!" don't turn. Sashay out the door, dragging the offensive portion of the quilt with you.

Pretend You're Suffering "Kitty Crazies." Vault into the room, jumping high like a bunny. As you caper over the quilt, hop sideways as if chasing your tail, then spin and slide like a mouser with paws outstretched. Finally, dash from the room, feet whirring like the wheels of Speed Racer. Do not reappear in the door until your human stops moaning, "Lookit this mess!"

Practice the Cat Firedrill. Pretend that your tail is on fire. With a howl, drop on to the quilt from a high ledge like a bookshelf, then roll so that patches flutter around you, dancing like kaleidoscope frames. Hop to your feet, skidding out the door, tail high, as your human groans, "Sometimes I think that animal needs kitty-Prozac."

Play the Magical Sphinx. Sit on an edge of the quilt. Quietly wrap your tail around you and close your eyes. Sit as still as an ancient statue. Sit so quietly that your human forgets that you're there. Eventually she will look away from her quilt in order to hunt for something in her sewing basket or paw through a stack of fabric. When she looks back her quilt will look like something from another world. But you will still be perched on its edge, eyes closed.

66 *My cat Percy knows when I am quilting. He has to sit right in front of me in the middle of all my fabrics. He sits on my lap while I machine quilt and he loves it when I make yo-yo's. Percy helped me pick the color scheme for my last quilt by sliding all across the fabric. Quilting bees are his passion!* 99

— LAURA GRASER, TAMAQUA, PENNSYLVANIA

Lesson #6 You Can Improve Floral Appliqués by Eating Them

What cat doesn't enjoy watching the delicate buds and leaves of an appliqué design unfurl from a human's hands and needle? What most cats don't realize is that rather than sitting passively on their human's lap during the stitching of floral quilt blocks, they can provide powerful artistic guidance.

The next time one of those leaves flutters off a muslin block, nab it with a paw and pop it in your mouth. Your human will likely gasp. She may poke a finger in your mouth and try to fish out the fabric. But do not give it up. Chew as fast as you can. Eventually she will rescue her leaf from your teeth, but by then it will be a soppy mess. She'll need to cut another leaf, which she will probably forget to do. This is how you can build your own artistic legacy. When she resumes stitching her flower, pull a loose petal or vine off the quilt top.

> " Every time I sit down at my sewing machine, one of my cats perches on the far side of the machine and paws at the thread or chews it. The other cat lays down between me and the machine to sleep. "
>
> — ANN SAYWELL, WINNIPEG, MANITOBA

Lesson #7   Select Your Quilt Batting Wisely

As a cat quilter you know instinctively that batting–or the cotton inside the quilt–is as critical a part of the quilt as its patched top. Who can sleep on a quilt padded with cotton that's as lumpy as the state of Montana? What cat can close his eyes in rhythmic reverie as his claws knead a quilt that's as stiff as the bottom of a litter tray?

Like Goldilocks in search of the perfect bed, you want blanket stuffing that is not too soft, not too hard, but is cozy enough to accommodate itself to the delicate curves of your sleeping feline form. In an ideal world your human would unroll numerous brands of cotton batting on the floor and allow you to nap on each to test them. But that is unlikely to happen.

So how can you select the perfect quilt bat under these less-than-ideal circumstances? Whenever you spot your human pulling something cottony from a bag, walk toward it quickly. Encourage her to set it down in front of you so that you may knead it with your paws. Close your eyes. Ask yourself: Is this too hard? Will I be able to sleep on this for many days without awakening with a stiff tail? If the batting feels soft, stretch out on it for the nap test. If your human is alert, when she spots you sleeping fitfully on her cotton, she will know that she has chosen the perfect stuffing for her quilt.

My tortoise shell kitty Tacy likes to steal sewing tools. She will knock tins of needles, rulers, and even scissors to the floor, then bat them around and hide them all over the house. She hooks a claw into them and scoots off with them. Her favorite toy is a brush I use to clean my sewing machine. No matter where I hide it, she finds it. Then she hides it from me. She also likes to sneak into piles of batting scraps to hide.

— BECKY VALCANTE

My kitten likes to sleep on my long-arm quilting machine as I'm quilting. When I'm loading a quilt on the machine, she plays under the material as if it were a tent. When I start to quilt, she retires to a corner to sleep.

— CAROL COOK, FORKS, WASHINGTON

Some years ago I was owned by a lovely long-haired black cat named Jedda. Jedda was always in my sewing room when I sewed. Jedda would find any dropped pins by picking them up and dropping them on the polished boards of the floor, making a tinkling sound, until I took them from her. She would find all the lost pins this way. When there were no more dropped pins, she would curl up on the spare bed to sleep. If I dropped another pin she would instantly awaken to retrieve it for me. I still miss this most wonderful and compassionate of cats!

—SHARYN BASSETT, QUEENSLAND, AUSTRALIA

CATS WHO QUILT

Lesson #8 — How to Assemble the Quilt Without Getting Stuck in It

When many cats start quilting, they make the mistake of crawling between the quilt's batting and its colorful patched top when the unfinished quilt is laid out on a floor or table for basting. They slowly wiggle their way to the center of the quilt. There they sit, believing themselves to be invisible because all they see around them is darkness. In reality, they look like a large lump that will need to be basted around. Humans who are as new to quilting as their cats are may do just that.

As your human is assembling the quilt, your main supervisory responsibility will be to ensure that nothing runs out of the quilt. What could run out of it? Dogs, for one. Dogs feel no compunctions about wiggling into a quilt, muddy paws and all. Rabbits have also been known to hop out of a quilt sandwich.

Patrol the quilt's perimeter. Keep a close eye on any lumps in case they should start moving. Occasionally slide a paw under the quilt to feel around. Should you feel anything suspicious, pounce on it. Should something inside the quilt run out, chase it. When you tire from this exertion, sashay across the top of the quilt. Drop to your side and stretch out for a well-deserved nap.

"*While I sew the binding on my quilt, my Tammy cat I'm sure thinks, 'Ah, another one she's making for me.'*"

— DONNA BROKENSHIRE, TROY, MICHIGAN

"*My cat Sam loves to walk on my fabric, my batting, and anything pertaining to my quilting. One day, as I stitched at the sewing machine, I noticed that the quilt felt heavy, but assumed it was because of my quilting. All of a sudden, a scream came from inside the rolled quilt. Out crawled a very angry and upset cat.*"

— MAGGIE TALYLOR, SILVER SPRING, MARYLAND

Lesson #9 Do Not Fall Off the Quilting Frame

At first glance, quilting frames look like the perfect diving board from which to spring to other high places, like a window ledge or sewing machine stand. But don't be deceived, for quilt frames' inherent structural unreliability makes them as dangerous to us cats as wobbly hammocks.

When a quilt frame falls over it makes a terrible clatter. It goes "Ker-clunk!" It will cause the fur on your back to bristle. If you are standing on the quilt frame when it topples, you will be thrown like a squirrel out of an upended bird feeder—that is unless your claws are fastened in the quilt, in which case you will invariably tumble over with it and land in an embarrassing pose. If other small creatures are present, they will scatter at the ruckus (but not without first laughing at you). If your human is within earshot she will blame you for knocking over the frame.

You can't win with quilt frames. Like dogs, they are ungainly, crazily designed, and bent upon making you look foolish. The only thing to do with one is to drag toys under it. As you drag your catnip mice, feather wands, and rattling balls under the quilt frame, pretend that you are a jungle predator dragging booty back to your cloaked lair. Should anyone venture near you, hiss. With a clawy paw, bat anyone who trifles with your toys.

Once your toys are heaped beneath the frame, guard them like a desert pasha protects the treasures in his tent. Sit quietly beneath the frame. Do not let anyone know you're there. Should a pair of feet intrude, restrain the urge to nip their ankles. Only if you spot something dangling over the edge of the frame–like a thread or hand—should you announce your presence by leaping for it.

Lesson #10 Tape Measure Aerobics

The concept of a tape measure is hard for most cats to understand. We cats do not measure things. Why measure something when one can simply chase it?

But you will not get far as a cat quilter if you do not know how to play with a tape measure. Oh sure, your quilts will still look like a hodgepodge of bedraggled calico patches, as other cats' quilts do. But you will not have enjoyed as fulfilling an artistic journey of self-discovery as you would have if you mangled a tape measure or two in the process.

How many tape measures should you shred while sewing a quilt? At least four or five. Here's how:

1. Pretend that the tape measure is a snake slithering away through the grass.

2. Crouch low to get it in your vision.

3. Leap up, pounce, and bat it fiercely. If it puts up a fight, nab it with your teeth and drag it under a chair. If the tape measure is dangling over the edge of the sewing machine, roll onto your back on the floor beneath and grab it between your paws. Bite and kick it so it does not wiggle away.

4. Once you have the tape measure under control, sit on it. If your human quilting partner tries to take it away, smack her with your paw and hiss until she backs away.

My cats, Bows and Clara, were thrilled when I put up my quilt frame to quilt the Star of Bethlehem quilt that was left to me when my husband's grandmother died. They thought it was a wonderful place to rest when nobody was around. We tried our best to keep them off the quilt, but the cats were determined to call it their new bed.

— DOREEN GRAHAM, COLD LAKE, ALBERTA

Cyrano de Burga-cat has been banished from my sewing room for his own good. Why? Because he steals. He steals material—yards and yards of it. He's very selective about the material he steals, though. I've found countless piles of fabric knocked to the floor, with one of the fabrics from the very middle of the pile missing. Cyrano usually pulls out fabric with a dark blue background. Sometimes he pulls out browns. If I find material missing from the sewing room, I search the house. I usually find it in Cyrano's current nest, which is whatever spot he's decided is most comfortable at the time. I worry that he'll hurt himself dragging all that fabric down the steps from my third-floor sewing room. He's ten years old, and, as with most coddled felines, is a large fellow.

—DEBRA SYZDEK, PHILADELPHIA, PENNSYLVANIA

What if your human is the type of quilter who meticulously folds her fabric and stacks it on shelves? Scale the fabric stack vertically, like a tree of many colors.

Lesson #11 Organizing Your Collection of Fabric

Human quilters are of contrary philosophies when it comes to organizing their fabrics. Some neatly fold and stack fabric on shelves in their sewing room, ordering it by colors. Others jam their scraps into a variety of bushel baskets, plastic bags, and Tupperware bowls that they stuff into the closet. They upend these like barrels of apples whenever they need to hunt for a fabric.

We cats prefer the latter type of quilter. One never knows, when supervising this sort of quilter, when she will pull out a basket of fabric, dump its contents on the floor, and begin frolicking in them, beckoning you to jump in. Prancing and hopping through such a disarray is more fun than playing in a pile of socks. One can be assured that it will take the human hours to pick up all the fabric and pack it back into the bags and baskets.

What if your human is the type of quilter who meticulously folds her fabric and stacks it on shelves? There is hope. Wait until she is asleep and the sewing room is dark. Hop up on a shelf and scale its fabric stack vertically, like a tree of many colors. With any luck, both you and the fabric will fall onto the floor, fabric scattering everywhere. This will give you many opportunities to play, experimenting with fabric patterns and colors until your human cleans up the mess.

Lesson #12 How to Pose With Your Quilt

Once your quilt is finished, you will need to find the best way to pose with it. Whether the quilt is draped over a bed or hangs from a wall, how you crouch on it or prance in front of it will determine the degree to which viewers admire you.

While it nearly goes without saying that you want to sit in front of the portion of the quilt that highlights the distinctive coloring and texture of your fur to their best advantage, you also want to create a mood by the pose that you strike. For instance, a cat crunched in the center of a bed with eyes closed and paws tucked under him inspires meditation. But a cat sitting on a cluttered cabinet, even with his quilt hanging behind him, may be mistaken for a piece of fleamarket bric-a-brac.

When you sit in front of your quilt, watch the reactions of humans who pass you. Do they notice you? Or do they ignore you and look at the quilt instead? Worse, do they rudely sniff, "You've been sitting in front of that quilt for hours. Don't you have something better to do?"

Here are a few suggestion to help you determine the best way to pose with your quilt:

Orange Tiger Cats: Few people take orange tiger cats seriously, especially those cats with potbellies. (Don't I know?) That's why tiger cats should stand in front of only serious-looking quilts, like Depression-era and Civil War quilts in grim colors. You should stay away from winsome pictorial quilts like those depicting children chasing balloons or teddy bears dancing. Pastels make you look fat.

Black Cats: Never ever sit on a quilt patched in a Halloween theme. A black cat perched on a quilt swarming with witches and goblins is an unspeakable cliché. You should also avoid quilts sewn in a country-decor theme, with tiny brown or orange calicos, which are reminiscent of Halloween. Instead, pose in front of art quilts with sleek contemporary lines, and sophisticated uses of color. Stand very still and straight like an elegant porcelain statue of a cat god.

Once your quilt is finished, you will need to find the best way to pose with it. If you are a black cat, stand in front of art quilts with sleek contemporary lines.

White Cats: With your lacey fur you can't go wrong sitting in front of a quilt festooned with floral appliqué. But be careful when you sit on a quilt that is spread on a bed. You don't want to look like some fluffy stuffed toy cat that a teenage girl plopped there. If you plan to lay on a bed, stick to ones with quilts patched in an oriental or Celtic design. Ivory cats also look lovely curled on bargello quilts patched in watercolor pastels, but be careful that there are no stuffed toy animals in the area or else you might be mistaken for one.

CATS WHO QUILT

Brown Cats With Mottled Stripes: Play up your brown and black stripes by sticking to poses that make you look tiger-like. Sit on the quilt with your head low against your paws, or else sit in front of it like a stone lion guarding the steps to an art museum, head erect, paws stretched in front of you. Try to pose with quilts patched with jungle themes or fabrics. Stay away from quilts with appliqué cows. With your coloring, you might be mistaken for one.

Gray Cats With White Paws: Thanks to your stylish fur, you will look charming standing in front of just about any quilt. But the higher the quilt hangs the better, because a sky-high backdrop will enhance your appearance of long-legged lithesomeness. Quilts draped over upper-level bunk bends and hanging from cathedral ceilings are perfect for white-pawed cats to pose against. But don't scale a quilt hanging from a high wall, then dangle from it by two paws and expect passersby to admire you. Maritime-themed quilts with lighthouses and life buoys make ideal backgrounds to your jaunty air.

If you are a lacey white cat, be careful when you lay on a quilt that is spread on a bed. You don't want to look like some fluffy stuffed toy cat that a teenage girl has dropped there.

A sewing basket is only as good as the
number of cats that can crawl into it.

The Laws of Cat Quilting

If it's not sewn down, chase it.

If it's not pinned down, chew it.

The closer you stay to a quilter's hands the more gentle caresses you will elicit.

If someone should try to pull the fabric out from under you, hold on tight.

Everything you step on is yours.

Never neglect an opportunity to get in the way.

There has never been a quilt that hasn't been improved by a cat sleeping on it.

A sewing basket is only as good as the number of cats that can crawl into it.

Thread is always more fun when it's tangled around something.

If it doesn't look right, sleep on it.

A Gallery of Cat Quilts

"Puss is involved in every log cabin quilt I make. He toys with the strips as they dangle from my machine and scrambles amid the finished squares as I lay them on the floor. He sits on the binding as I try to pin it and he sleeps in the batting."

— JACQUELINE GWYNNE, CHICAGO, ILLINOIS

One rarely sees quilts created by cats hanging in art galleries. Cats' painstaking handiwork is often dismissed by unenlightened humans as having "stitching teased by cat claws" or being "calico spotted with spit-up cat food." Some people even feel the need to invent excuses for their cats' cleverness. "I guess my kitty got into mischief as I was sewing the quilt together," they'll mumble when someone points out the cat claw ripping through the flying geese border or the fur ball shining forth from the Navajo Star.

That's why I have assembled this collection of cat-created quilts. I know you will be as inspired as I have by such wondrous confections as Dizzy Johnny's Sunbonnet Bert and the Cat Tree—are those cat tails spinning or is that really a Welsh corgi falling off a carpet-covered cat tree? I think you will marvel too at the stories of some of the intrepid cat quilters—like Big Flo, who continues quilting even when she feels an overpowering urge to nap.

If you are a human, I hope you take heart: one day you too could be sewing quilts like these. But first, you must get down on your hands and knees and let your cat show you how quilting really should be done.

Twinkle Tess, Bumblebees-in-a-Hurry, and Wings-a-Flutter

Sometimes her quilts look like nothing but scattered fabric patches. Indeed, Twinkle herself—named after her light-footed "twinkletoes"—admits that some of her quilts have required less than thirty seconds to assemble. That's all the time she needs, she says, to run into her human's sewing room, scamper over the quilt, and race out the door. Although the exhausted artist occasionally returns to the sewing room to sit in the center of the quilt and howl pitifully for something to eat, she prefers to let the patches fall where they may. On most days she leaves the whole mess to her human assistant to sew together.

Wings-a-Flutter is Twinkle's interpretation of what Kansas Dugout quilt blocks would look like if pigeons were to weave them into a nest and scatter them on balconies. Bumblebees-in-a-Hurry reflects her struggle to depict what a Log Cabin quilt would look like if one threw it over a picnic table, spilled a can of Diet Pepsi on it, and let the bumblebees carry it off.

Tess believes that in the future other animals besides cats will quilt—ostriches, for example. She believes that if other species were only given the opportunity to run into a sewing room and run out, great art could be achieved.

Twinkle Tess enjoys letting the patches fall where they may. She believes it's important to have a human quilting assistant who will clean up after any intensively creative quilting session.

Dizzy Johnny a.k.a. "Lotsa Toes" & Sunbonnet Bert and the Cat Tree

Dizzy Johnny scoffs at any suggestion that he is a quilter, but visit the home of the Babbalaws in Marvella, Kansas any Sunday evening and you will find Mrs. Babbalaw hunched over a quilt frame, stitching, as she watches TV. Meanwhile, her scrawny black cat Dizzy Johnny spins around her feet under the frame.

Why does Johnny spin? Sometimes he chases his tail. Sometimes he pretends he is possessed. Sometimes he thinks he's being chased in circles by an invisible cat, whom he occasionally stops to hiss at. Perhaps he is being chased by the spirit of a cat quilter who nuzzled whatever feet rested beneath Mrs. Babbalaw's used quilt frame in generations past.

Occasionally when Johnny stops spinning, he crawls into Mrs. Babbalaw's lap and growls grumpily when her rough hands attempt to scoop him out.

Dizzy Johnny's most famous quilt, Sunbonnet Bert and the Cat Tree, appears to depict a Welsh corgi—though one cannot be entirely sure—in a sunbonnet falling off a carpeted cat tree. The quilt originally began as an appliqué portrait of Grandma Babbalaw rocking in a chair on a farmhouse porch. But Mrs. Babbalaw claims that her cat Johnny so often scurried over her lap while she was stitching it that Grandma Babbalaw ended up looking like a Welsh corgi, and the rocking chair's legs grew architecturally reminiscent of a tilting cat tree.

Fortunately for Mrs. Babbalaw, her disheveled stitching is now one of cat quilting's greatest legacies.

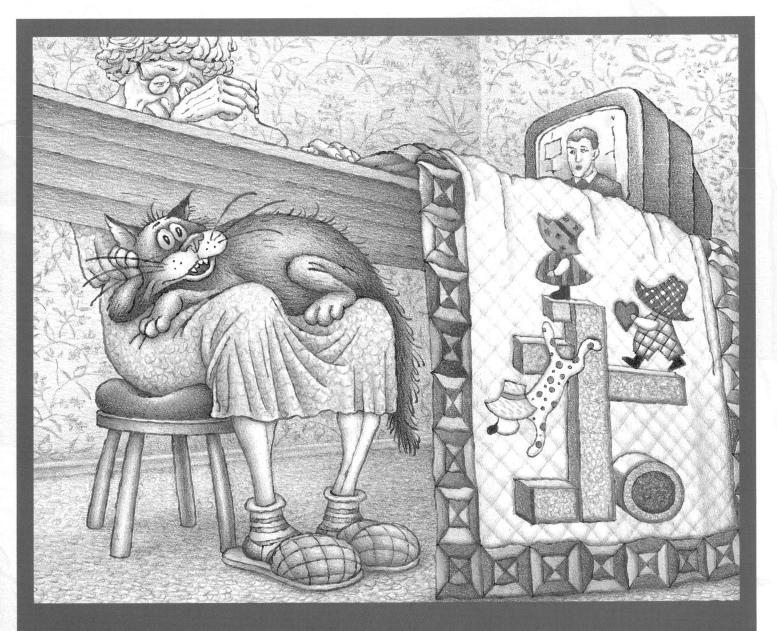

Dizzy Johnny's most famous quilt depicts a Welsh corgi in a sunbonnet falling off a carpeted cat tree.

Big Flo & Sunrise Over Nap Time

In cat quilting, body language is everything. No one knows this better than Big Flo, the porcupine-sized queen of the Ohio Star. Whenever her human's quilting guild assembles, all the quilters stop their work and fall silent, their needles poised in the air, as Big Flo sashays into the room. Everyone wonders where the striped cat will take her seat, whether her heavy paws will plod over the Nine-Patch border, whether her feathery tail will send the Mexican Roses fluttering, or if she will simply plop her lumpy body down amid the Tumbling Stars and wash her toes.

Big Flo begins every quilting session with a nap. And that's how she ends it as well. Sometimes she crawls into an open Craft Book of the Month Club tote bag to snooze away the hours as the ladies stitch. Is it any surprise that Big Flo's most famous quilt is a visual panegyric to somnambular self-indulgence?

Sunrise Over Nap Time is a festival of buttercup-colored patches depicting sunlight embracing a corpulent, sleeping cat. Sunshine kisses the tufted tips of the ears, dapples the rounded, furry back, and drips like honey down the curled, resting tail. But metaphor and life blur in dazzling visual repartee where beams of sunlight halo the frowzy head of the sleeping grimalkin as if it has been bestowed with sainthood. The word "snore" is embroidered lavishly around the whiskers. Emotionally moving as Sunrise Over Nap Time is, Big Flo has also imbued it with humor. Bits of cat food are stuck in the sleeping cat's whiskers. And some of them are real.

Big Flo begins every quilting session with a nap. Sometimes she crawls into a Craft Book of the Month Club tote bag to sleep as the ladies of her quilting guild stitch.

Pickles and Fur & What Stupid Dogs: The Imagery Continues

Derided as the "bullies of the cat quilting world," Pickles and Fur got their start quilting by chasing the family dogs, Blossom and Nuggetbrain, off a quilt-covered bed where the mutts had been sleeping. Some call these brothers' quilts "unnecessarily grim," for most depict dogs doing something doggedly stupid.

In Dogs Around the World dogs are depicted running in circles chasing empty plastic bleach bottles around tiny square patches. In Where Did All the Fur Go? A Nine-Patch Legacy, a large hound is shown cowering under a woman's patched skirt. Quilt lovers claim that the fur coating the disordered Nine Patch blocks is not that of the two cats, but fur shed in hysteria by pooches the cats have chased out of their sewing room and terrorized by hissing and ear-cuffing. In answer to criticism, the cats claim that they are merely reflecting in their quilts the grim reality that not every creature is as dapper, witty, and sophisticated as a cat.

In their latest opus, What Stupid Dogs: The Imagery Continues, Pickles and Fur have pieced the silhouettes of two long-eared mutts bouncing up and down in front of a window, barking at nothing in particular. Detractors claim that this time the cats have gone too far—the quilt looks like dogs have indeed been bouncing on it, as evidenced by all the muddy paw prints blotching the trapunto. The cats, in their defense, claim they are not responsible for hand-quilting blundered by subcontractors.

Pickles and Fur got their start quilting by chasing the family dogs off a quilt-covered bed. Some call these cats' quilts "grim," since most depict dogs doing something doggedly stupid.

Liza & Blue Cat Moon Adventure

 Liza, a lithesome creature with long white legs and wide eyes, likes to imbue her quilts with romance and a sense of adventure. It is often hard to see where her human's handiwork leaves off and Liza's influence begins; her quilting methods are as subtle as she is delicate. Quiet and light-footed as a sprite, she runs into the sewing room and hops on to her human's lap. Her favorite quilting technique is to rub her cheek against the hands of the human quilter as her mistress sews or pins. But after only moments, her human will pluck Liza from her lap with one hand and deposit her on the floor. Liza will run off, work done.

Only later will her human step back and, surveying the cat leaping over the moon or the clowder of cats basking in the glow of rustically pieced stars, marvel, "Why, Liza! I think you made me stitch that, didn't you?"

In Blue Cat Moon Adventure, Liza combines the excitement of chenille with the tension of sloppily cut felt to portray a cat flying after a can of cat food that has only recently discovered that it has wings and that it can use them to flee.

Liza's favorite quilting technique is to rub her cheek against the hands of her human quilter as the quilter sews or pins.

James "Tigger" Katerfelt-o & Why Is There Calico in My Tuna?

The most renowned of the cat "art quilters," James—or Tigger as his human quilting assistant calls him—has been toiling over the same quilt for most of his life. His human quilting assistant, Jessica, a large-lapped woman who has not cleaned out her sewing basket since the birth of the plastic canvas embroidery craze in 1974, has also been struggling to complete the quilt for most of her adult life as well. She claims she cannot finish it because Tigger keeps sprawling on it. (Most human quilters labor under the delusion that their cat's quilt is their quilt. Some even believe that they own their cat. A few wise up eventually, realizing that they are the ones who are enslaved. Fortunately, few reveal the details of their enslavement, fearing that other people will laugh at them.)

Tigger, who likes to stay close to his work, often carries mouthfuls of cat food from his dish by the kitchen sink into the bedroom where the quilt is laid on the floor. He spits the food on the quilt top and slowly munches it, bit by bit. This work pattern was the inspiration behind his career-making quilt Why Is There Calico in My Tuna? A celebration of spit-up fur balls and crumbs of meat by-products, the quilt was originally intended as a miniature bargello wall hanging for the guest powder room. Thanks to Tigger's efforts, it was vacuumed off and now serves as a potholder. Though bedraggled, the quilt is a legend that lives on in the annals of cat quilting.

Tigger's current work-in-progress is rumored to contain lots of Flying Geese blocks in which the geese look like they've been ambushed at a bird feeder.

Tigger likes to stay close to his work. He carries mouthfuls of cat food from his dish by the kitchen sink into the bedroom where his mistress quilts. This work pattern was the inspiration behind his career-making quilt Why Is There Calico In My Tuna?

Lollipop & Wedding Ring With a Cat

 Lollipop, a long-tailed fairy of a cat, is the happiest cat in the world—until her mistress's new husband, Frankenmuth, comes home at night. Frankenmuth carries a long, dark brief-case. Lollipop is convinced that in it he carries all the dishes of cat food he has stolen from her. (Why else would he pick up the dishes of dried cat food from the floor each morning and drop them into the sink if he didn't plan to steal them?) Frankenmuth throws cat toys like a sissy. Frankenmuth smells like insecticide after he takes a shower in the morning.

At night, as Frankenmuth sleeps, Lollipop climbs on to his chest and tries to steal his moustache. One time, she clamped a paw on to his nose and nearly prevented him from breathing for three seconds. Another time she scratched his scalp, and it developed into an infection for which he had to get shots. Often, along with the hair she pulls from his moustache, she also pulls out other things, like his sideburns. Sometimes Frankenmuth jerks awake at night scream-ing, as Lollipop races from the room, mouth full of hair.

In the morning, Frankenmuth stands staring into the mirror. He despairs that he is balding early.

All of these bits of Frankenmuth find their way into Lollipop's quilts, which can be described as explorations of female despair at having to live with a man who does not know how to throw cat toys properly. To the untrained eye, Lollipop's quilts look like any other quilt one might see covering a bed or hang-ing in a quilt shop window—a Wedding Ring quilt or a Log Cabin one. But shine a black light on them and one will detect, tucked beneath their surface fabric, storehouses of moustache hair and even a stolen sock or two.

Relics of Frankenmuth find their way into Lollipop's quilts, which can be described as explorations of female despair at having to live with a man who does not know how to throw cat toys properly.

Mr. Snuggles & Folk Art Wasn't Meant for the Innocent

Mr. Snuggles, a corpulent gray and black candy-cane striped cat with a sinister mien, spends his days sleeping beside the pillow of a woman with a festering illness. Sometimes, in the night, she pulls herself from her bed and hobbles to her sewing machine. Mr. Snuggles, jiggly striped belly swinging side to side, slogs after her. Hunched over her sewing machine, she pieces together quilts that begin innocently enough with a patched star or an appliquéd heart.

But she soon tires. As her fingers and sewing machine needle slow, Mr. Snuggles, crunched at her feet like a solemn rascal, sets to work. With deft slashes of his scythe-like claws, he transforms bright folk art-inspired quilt blocks into dark Hitchcockian scenes. His mistress is too tired to pick up the thirty-pound tabbycat and lug him from the room. She also knows that if she does he will sashay back, grumbling at his unfair eviction. So Mr. Snuggles, undisturbed, sometimes labors till dawn on his quilts. He bats patches and teases out thread, transforming innocent paper-pieced objects like fish and antique cars into dark totems of his jungle-predator vision.

In Folk Art Wasn't Meant for the Innocent, millions of black silk birds descend upon a gentle folk art-style village while Overall Bill crawls up a nearby church steeple to save a suicidal Sunbonnet Sue in a kitschy, patchwork rendition of a scene from Alfred Hitchcock's Vertigo.

The quilt was banned from juried exhibition at Pawducah after a dead starling fell out of the haphazardly stitched border. Mr. Snuggles defended his work by tearing his quilt off the wall, kneading it into a pile on the floor, and taking a nap on it in front of horrified onlookers.

With deft slashes of his scythe-like claws, Mr. Snuggles transforms bright folk art-inspired quilts into dark totems of his jungle predator vision.

Suzy, the Cat Angel & Feather Toys of Heaven

 Jean Hollack claims that she doesn't have a cat—not anymore. But sometimes when she is quilting late at night, after everyone else in the house is asleep, she catches, in a corner of her eye, a glimmer of a cat tail waving in a shadow of her sewing room. Or she hears the click of toenails padding over the wooden floor, stepping toward her. Sometimes she even thinks she hears a soft meow. But Jean knows she is mistaken, because she doesn't have a cat, not anymore.

When Jean's cat Suzy was alive, the tiny cat would perch like a guardian angel behind her shoulder, on the back of the couch. Or Suzy would lay across the couch back, with one delicate paw touching Jean's shoulder as she stitched. Sometimes Jean thinks the cat is still sitting there, a long velvet, patchy-colored paw stretched out, touching her shoulder.

Jean has recently completed a quilt which confirms this belief. A crazy quilt, like the ones Suzy especially liked to lie on because she liked the feel of the different patched velvets and cool silks against her thinly furred belly, its dark, uneven fabrics resemble Suzy's mottled-colored fur. It is striated with feather stitches. Wild, flamboyant feather stitches plume and curl everywhere in many different colors.

She calls it Feather Toys of Heaven. She thinks it is Suzy's way of telling her that heaven is full of feather toys that wave and dance for playful cat spirits like her to bat at. And she is right.

When Jean's cat Suzy was alive the tiny cat would perch like a guardian angel behind her shoulder, on the back of the couch, as Jean quilted. Sometimes Jean thinks Suzy is still there, watching over her.

How to Nap on a Quilt

"I am a quilter who is owned by a large albino cat named Saul. He doesn't like me to quilt, because he doesn't like the noise of the sewing machine, but also because he doesn't like anything that takes my attention away from His Royal Catness. He will bat my foot with his paw to get it off the machine pedal, or try to coax me away from the quilting frame. He will sleep under quilts with the best of them."

— ANNA CRANDELL,
SEVILLA, SPAIN

Cats often write to ask, "Clancy, what's the best way to nap on a quilt?" You might be surprised that a cat would ask for advice on how to sleep, but we cats are perfectionists. We take pride in our ability to find the warmest, coziest spot in the house to nap and to sleep there for long hours. It is this special talent, perhaps more than any other, which has led to our success as a species. Humans should follow our example.

But we cats are social sleepers. There is nothing we enjoy more than a fourteen-hour nap with a pal who requires the same. Through my rich life I have been fortunate to live with an elderly invalid, several colicky children frequently bed-bound with coughs and sneezes, and a young man whose idea of domestic bliss revolved around crawling beneath covers to snore his lonely nights away. All proved excellent sleep partners—and life partners as well.

In this chapter I will tell you how to find your perfect bed partner. I will also answer questions that we cats often have about sleeping on quilts, and how to make the most of the opportunity.

"Should I crawl under the quilt, or should I sleep on top of it?"

How Will I Know Which Quilt in the House to Sleep on? And Will There Be Pins in It When I Lie on It?

Even if there are many quilts in the house, you will be drawn to the softest one instinctively, as if by cat ESP. It will call to you like mermaids sing to lost sailors. Come to me, oh, beautiful, yawning cat! Come sleep on me for I am the finest and most cozy blanket in the house! it will whisper. Not only will it be the most comfy quilt on which to stretch your long, tired body, but it will be the one that the mistress of the house least wants you to lie on, for it will be the one that she has spent the most time and expense sewing. It will be the one she has arranged so carefully on a bed that it and the bed are together a work of art, a paean to Martha Stewart hominess.

Best of all, quilt and bed will probably be adorned with white lacey, fluffed-up pillows that you can knead with your paws and dishevel. There may be a quilt hanging over the bed as well, which you may climb, claw, or rip off the wall in order to work off the remainder of your playful energy before you settle into your nap.

Will pins be stuck in the quilt? Probably not, for you should have batted them all out and chased them across the floor when the quilt was still under construction.

> **66** *My cat Cricket is deaf, but he loves to sleep where he can feel my sewing machine vibrating. His favorite place is in the window above my sewing table, where he can feel the vibration through the wall.* **99**
> — SHARON HOLLIDAY, GARLAND, TEXAS

62 **CATS WHO QUILT**

How Long Should I Knead the Quilt with My Claws Before Curling in It to Sleep?

Knead the quilt until it reminds you of your mother's soft embrace. Close your eyes and press your paws into it until lowering your tired body into the fabric folds feels just like curling against your mother's downy chest. Many humans also believe that this is the way that quilts should feel before they lay on them. Unfortunately, a human mother's chest is often bejeweled with buttons, zippers, collars, and cameo broaches. Make sure that if there are any of these sewn into your quilt you do not lie on them.

Should I Crawl Under the Quilt, or Should I Sleep on Top?

That depends upon whether you're allowed to lay on the quilt or not. It will also depend upon whether your human quilting partner will grow suspicious if she spots a large blanket lump inching across her carefully arranged bed. However, if the sun is beaming warmly across the bed, by all means sleep on top the quilt, regardless of whether you'll be tossed off when you're spotted. It will be worth it.

Should I Let My Human Sleep With Me on the Quilt?

Again, it depends. If the human tosses as he sleeps, I would advise not. Also, if the human possesses an alarm clock, he should be required to sleep on the porch.

However, if the human habitually carries tuna sandwiches to bed and eats them under the covers, you should definitely permit him to sleep on the quilt with you, even if he has an alarm clock.

Do You Have Other Advice for Selecting Humans to Sleep With Me on My Quilt?

Look for older women who have toiled long and hard in life and appreciate a good nap—and the contentment that comes from having a warm cat curled asleep at one's feet.

Look for small children who will not tell their parents that you have snuck into their bedroom and hopped on the bed, but will simply giggle and fall asleep.

Look for people who are having a tough lot in life. When you walk over them as they slumber, they will think you are trying to nurse them. When you squawk they will think you are trying to cheer them. When they recover cheerfully, they will assign all credit to you, and never remove you from their bed again.

Avoid anyone who stands on her bed in her stocking feet and jumps up and down.

Are There Dangers in Letting a Human Sleep on My Quilt?

There are the obvious ones like fleas and ear mites. But the greatest danger is that the human might come to regard the quilt as hers, when it is really yours.

Is there a way to prevent this? Yes. Try to spend at least 95 percent of your life sleeping on the quilt. When any human approaches, bare your fangs and hiss. Another tactic is to permit only a select member of the household to sit on the quilt beside you. For instance, I know cats who will permit the missus to sleep on the quilt with them, but will arch themselves into a Halloween cat when the mister steps near the bed.

If the quilt is draping a guest-room bed, you have your work cut out for you. On the one hand, turning the hands and ankles of houseguests into cat ragout is a sure way to find yourself locked in the basement for the night. On the other hand, it's your quilt and you need to defend it from ungainly squatters, especially those who might not arrange the pillows properly in the morning.

One effective technique is to stand outside the guest room door, mewing and scratching it all night. An even more effective technique: When bare-footed guests emerge in the morning, chase them, hissing and spitting, all the way to the bathroom. When they have locked the bathroom door behind them, after fighting you off with a towel, return to your place on top the quilt and refuse to budge until the interlopers' suitcases are removed.

How About Other Animals?

No, no, no! If other animals craws on the quilt, they should be chased off immediately.

What if They Crawl Back on?

Remind them politely that you are a descendant of the Egyptian cat goddess Bastet—then fly at them howling.

How Often Should I Rearrange Myself on the Quilt During My Nap?

As many times as possible. By the time you are finished with your nap the quilt should look as if the shape of a feline body was molded into it by design. By the end of your first week of slumbering on it, the quilt it should look as rumpled as if newly pulled from the leaves and twigs of a primordial cat den.

CATS WHO QUILT

What Is the Optimal Length of a Nap on a Quilt?

You want to snooze long enough to enjoy enough pleasant dreams to erase the world's ugliness (like the appalling visage of that dog bouncing outside your window).

You want to dream long enough so that the sunlight shifts from one corner of the room to another, giving you the sense that much time has passed, but it has not been wasted.

You want to sleep long enough that when you awaken, you're either hungry or ready to play. Both of these urges make life worth living again after one has been felled by exhaustion.

What Should I Dream About When Sleeping on a Quilt?

Dream about days when cats rode round the Egyptian sun
As gods and goddesses; dream about
Days when cats pulled Freya's chariot,
And helped turn Diana into the moon.
Dream about chasing bumblebees.
Or gamboling through blowing wildflowers.
Dream about thread that tangles around your tail,
And sewing baskets that upend to reveal marvelous toys;
Dream about chasing gophers around drainpipes
Dream about all the things that make you happy,
Like soft voices and hands that scoop you up
As you weave around a friend's ankles, and she tells you
Secrets and dreams as she flicks your ears,
Strokes your tail, rubs your back, and nestles you
Close into her lap, tight to her heart,
As she quilts.

How to Teach a Human to Quilt Like a Cat

"When my Siamese cat, Bashful, sees me getting things ready to quilt, he's up on the table, checking out all the fabric, looking for the most comfortable piece to lie on. He helps me through every phase—cutting, sewing, layering, pinning, and quilting. He also sits on the sewing machine as I piece a quilt."

— JAN SCOTT

For humans, learning to quilt like a cat is a long and difficult process. Indeed, for most, learning to quilt like a human is hard enough. They take classes, they buy books, they rent videos. Still, they crunch on the couch each night brandishing a quilting hoop as awkwardly as if it were a buggy wheel. They stab fabric with a clenched needle, their glasses sliding down their nose. Their fist is tight around the quilting hoop. No matter how they sigh and wrestle with the fabric, their Drunkard's Path blocks still look decidedly drunken.

As a cat quilter, you can't help but feel sad for them. You feel sad for them because they don't have tails. Because they don't, they struggle around on the floor on their hands and knees, their fingers grasping a pin-cushion as awkwardly as if it were a bowling ball. Because they don't have tails they can't fly over a quilt like a squirrel, as we do. You also feel sad for them because, when they jump up and down in frustration, they don't always land gracefully on their toes like we do. Most wear shoes that are heavy enough to flatten a pecan tree were they and their shoes to roll down a mountainside. This makes it hard for them to kick quilt patches with their toes.

But saddest of all are the humans who do not tire easily enough to be good quilters. We cats fall asleep almost instantly wherever we lie. That, my friends, is the secret talent which makes cats such great quilters! We know quality in a quilt the moment we fall asleep on it.

If you want to teach a human how to quilt like a cat, you have your work cut out for you. Here are some strategies:

Communicate With the Struggling Quilter by Cat ESP

The most effective way to show a human how to quilt is to climb over her lap, meowing encouragements, while batting her earrings, snagging her thread, and chewing on her sleeve. When your human attempts to push you out of her lap, complaining, "You know, it's not easy sewing with a fat cat sitting in my lap," communicate with her via telepathy: "It may not be easy sewing with a cat in your lap, but believe you me, babe, it's better than sewing with an orangutan in your lap."

When your human complains, "Everything I sew does not necessarily benefit from being flattened by a cat butt," and gropes under your tail for her sewing gear, she is actually responding to the stress of quilting. Remind her with plaintive meows that although her stitching may not be good enough to tack together a dog bed, it's her effort that counts. She will eventually come to her senses. She will retract her previous insult. She will say something like, "My dear cat, what I meant to say is you work much too hard sitting on and flattening everything I sew. Please take a nap. I can always use the steam iron later."

When your human grumbles, "You've been sitting on the same spot on my quilt for half the day, staring into space. Don't you have anything better to do?" communicate with her via ESP: "I am working on my artistic focus. Don't you wish you had some?"

When your human snatches the tape measure from between your paws, do not grow disheartened. Patiently communicate with her via cat ESP: "Please give me back the tape measure, dear, so that I can continue to show you how to smack it around the floor and pretend it is a dead worm. This is an advanced quilting technique. You will never learn it if you keep taking the tape measure from me."

There is no problem in art (or life) that cannot be solved by laying down in the middle of everything and taking a nap.

When your human attempts to push you out of her lap, complaining, "You know, it's not easy sewing with a fat cat sitting in my lap," communicate to her via telepathy: "It may not be easy sewing with a cat in your lap, but believe you me, babe, it's better than sewing with an orangutan in your lap."

Why Humans Cannot Quilt as Well as Cats Can....

They don't have tails.

It's difficult for them to pretend they are other creatures like squirrels and monkeys when they fall off sewing machines.

When they see a lovely quilt, they don't instantly fall asleep on it, like we do.

They are too big to wiggle inside a sewing basket.

They can't mew sadly whenever they want to stop working and eat a cat treat.

They don't see the invisible fairies like we do.

"If, while climbing over your human's lap, she should cry out as if stabbed, and gasp, 'I think your claws need trimming!' run off as fast as you can!"
—CLANCY

> My kitty definitely quilts. She helps me remove straight pins from the quilt and deposits them in a corner. When I'm arranging blocks on the floor, she moves them around to suit her taste and she'll go to my piles of fabric and select those she wants me to use.
— SOPHIA HOEFER

Ten Easy Things that You as a Cat Can Do to Improve a Quilt

1. You can gambol across it.

2. You can roll on top it.

3. You can eat it.

4. You can bat its patches into the air and imagine they are birds.

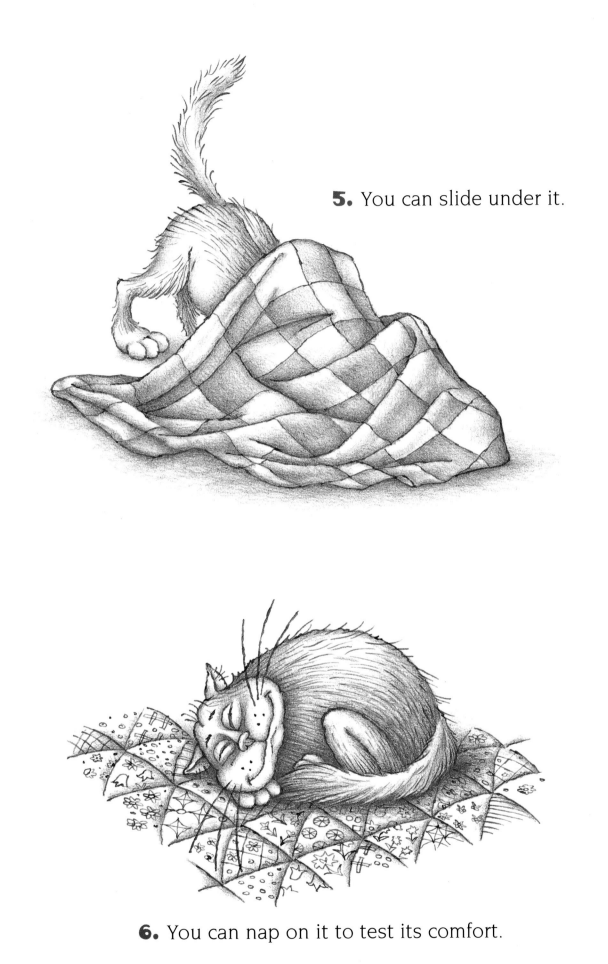

5. You can slide under it.

6. You can nap on it to test its comfort.

7. You can push it off the edge of the sewing machine and watch it fall on the floor.

8. You can drag it off like prey.

9. You can stare at it.

10. You can sit on it until someone chases you away.

More Tricks for Cats Who Quilt

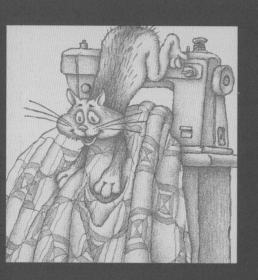

> "When we have houseguests, I have to warn them about Mr. Smokey. Each morning when I make the beds, he makes a bee-line up the stairs. He loves to wrestle in the quilts. When I smooth the sheets, he hunches down by the quilt. I throw the quilt over him. Sometimes he flops over on his back with all fours skyward. I play with him when he's under the quilt."
>
> — MARILYN JEWELL, CONCORD, NEW HAMPSHIRE.

In cat quilting contests, cats earn points for the number of patches that they can sit on.

Quilting Contests for Cats

Cats enjoy quilting contests as much as humans do. How do cats hold quilting contests? By sitting on quilts. The first step is to get as many cats as possible to sit on the quilt. This is easily done if many cats live in your household. Once all the cats are sitting on the quilt, they earn points for the number of patches in the quilt that they can walk on, crawl over, or lay on. Scores are communicated to other cats by blinks and tail twitches. Cats lose points by chasing other cats off the quilt. Extra points are earned if sunlight touches any cat while she is sitting on the quilt. The game is over if a dog jumps on the bed.

Wearable Art for Cats

Face it, pink-satin, pet-boutique jackets get old fast. Being a cat, you understand the importance of style. Who else but a cat can prance into a room with his ears tilted in that jaunty fashion that announces, "Look! Fur person approaching!" Wearable art is as close as your fabric basket. Simply bat around a few spools of thread, upend a button basket, unravel a zipper or two—and poof! You've created a fashion statement that Isaac Mizrahi's cat would be proud of.

"Silly you! You always wanted to be the Cat in the Hat —but you never realized it was this simple."

"Do you jiggle around the middle? Sleeken your physique with a patchwork coat that covers you in all the right places."

"A stylish cape could be just the thing to cover that nylon collar with the rabies vaccination tag."

Sewing Machine Attachments and What They Mean to You as a Cat Quilter

They look like miniature cat food can openers. Alas, their purpose is more prosaic. They are sewing machine attachments, or knobby implements that your human screws to her sewing machine in order to perform different sorts of stitching.

Sewing machine attachments are normally stored in a small box in a drawer of the sewing machine's cabinet. Your human quilter will likely remove this box from the drawer while sewing. She will open it. She will pull out a presser foot or machine-embroidery guide. She will attach it to her sewing machine, and sew with it. Then she will detach the implement and attach another one.

While she is doing this, take the opportunity to inspect the box carefully and examine the small tools inside. Only when you have completely familiarized yourself with the sewing machine attachments, and assured yourself that none could be used to open a can of cat food, should you knock the box off the sewing machine and watch its contents scatter across the floor.

Presser Foot: This the standard sewing machine foot. It holds down the fabric as the quilter feeds the cloth through the sewing machine. Think of a presser foot as if it were a cat foot holding down a gopher in order to prevent it from running off. When you smack a presser foot across the floor it will slide a long distance, and sometimes even spin. You can chase it and pretend it is a grasshopper and no one will question your sanity. A presser foot is best hidden under a rug.

Zipper Foot: Seamstresses use these to sew in place zippers and stitch other tight seams. But an even better use that you can put them to is to push them off the edge of a sewing machine and watch them hit the floor with a 'Clunk!' A zipper foot is best hidden under a chair.

Free-motion Embroidery Foot: This sewing machine foot often has a plastic scythe that you can chew on and break. When it's attached to the sewing machine it exhibits a spring-like quality that makes it even easier to break. An embroidery foot is best hidden in a shoe.

Hemmer: You will recognize the hemmer by the fact that it has a lot of places on which you can catch your claws. Hemmers tend to easily vanish under quilts, tables, and beds. You can easily pick them up in your mouth and carry them off. A hemmer is best hidden behind curtains.

"I once tried to open a can of cat food with a sewing machine presser foot, but did not get very far."

"Some years ago I was owned by a lovely long-haired black cat named Jedda. Jedda was always in my sewing room when I sewed. Jedda would find any dropped pins by picking them up and dropping them on the polished boards of the floor, making a tinkling sound, until I took them from her. She would find all the lost pins this way. When there were no more dropped pins, she would curl up on the spare bed to sleep. If I dropped another pin she would instantly awaken to retrieve it for me. I still miss this most wonderful and compassionate of cats!"

— SHARYN BASSETT,
QUEENSLAND, AUSTRALIA

"I love the silhouetted illustrations of cats on cat litter bags. I've used them for appliqués in two quilts already."

— JENNIFER NEIGHBOURS,
ORO VALLEY, ARIZONA

"My tortoise shell kitty Tacy likes to steal sewing tools. She will knock tins of needles, rulers, and even scissors to the floor, then bat them around and hide them all over the house. She hooks a claw into them and scoots off with them. Her favorite toy is a brush I use to clean my sewing machine. No matter where I hide it, she finds it. Then she hides it from me. She also likes to sneak into piles of batting scraps to hide."

— BECKY VALCANTE

"Pumpkin is my quilting cat. He likes to sit on the top of my sewing machine and often reaches down to adjust the tread tension when he—and only he—perceives there is a problem."

— BEV

How to Fix a Human's Quilting Mistakes With Hairballs

No human can sew a perfect quilt. Even humans' best efforts are flawed by jags of uneven stitching and puckers of fabric. Why not help your human quilting friend hide her embarrassing quilting mistakes? In the process you can put to use a perfectly good hairball that might otherwise end up in a vacuum cleaner bag. When no one is looking, scamper onto the quilt. You want to spit up the hairball in a spot where it won't be found for several weeks. That way the hairball will form a tight, semi-permanent bond with the fabric and will be hard to scrape off. Once you are sitting on the quilt, crouch down. Act nonchalant. Lower your head as if you are watching a bug. Cough slightly. Twitch your tail. Then spit out the hairball. Run away as fast as you can. If the hairball has been successfully applied, it will dry onto the fabric as if it was a felt-like plaster, unyielding to stain remover, wash cloth, or blow torch.

The Hairball Rule of Cat Quilting: "A hairball, once successfully applied to a quilt, will go undetected until the quilt has been entered in a quilt contest, is given as a gift to a testy in-law or peevish head-of-state, or an esteemed guest is burrowing beneath the quilt, preparing to fall into happy slumber."

"My slogan is a quilt is not a quilt without a few cat hairs."

— GAIL D. CROWE, MOCKSVILLE, NORTH CAROLINA

" Several years ago, I was upstairs cutting out quilt pieces with a rotary cutter. My long-haired tortoiseshell cat Dust Bunny flopped down on the cutting board. I didn't see that long fluffy tail, and sliced off two inches of fur, although fortunately I missed the tail itself. She apparently didn't notice, and lay there washing her face and purring. But I had to sit down in a chair because I was shaking so. "

— JOY BRANHAM, EIDSON, TENNESSEE

" My Mr. Smokey, a Russian Blue who rules the house, knows when there's a quilt in progress, about to be cut out, sewn, appliquéd, you name it. There he is in the middle of everything. There will never a quilt made in this house that is free of his little gray hairs. He loves my quilts and I love him. A match made in heaven. "

— MARILYN JEWELL, CONCORD, NEW HAMPSHIRE

" My only attempt at quilting to date, a small cat-theme wall-hanging, was layed out on the bed for layering and basting. Maxwell Murphy O'Shagnessy, cat blarney artist extraordinaire, took over the arrangement of quilt batting. To distract him, I had to give him his own piece of batting to play with so that I could arrange the batting my way. A fair amount of his fur is now quilted inside the quilt. "

— KAREN PAULI, MILWAUKEE, WISCONSIN

88 CATS WHO QUILT

Improve Surface Embellishment by Sitting on It

"Surface embellishment" is quilting parlance for anything stuck on top a quilt. This includes ribbons, lace, buttons, decorative stitching, shoe-strings, and gum. Spit-up cat food also falls into this category. The problem with surface embellishment, from a cat's vantage, is that it's often unpleasant to sit on. In fact, it's usually pretty lumpy.

What can you do about it? As cats we know that a quilt's purpose is served only if we are sleeping on it. If ribbons or bows are poking you in the belly as you settle onto a quilt for a nap, all you need do to remedy your discomfort is to take a moment to sit on the offensive gewgaws until they flatten. You'll find that stiff ribbons will flatten like limp marshmallows if you roll around on top of them. Even the scratchiest hand-stitching will disappear in folds of fabric if pressured to do so by a sufficiently luxuriant cat derriere.

This only goes to show that there is no element in the art world that will not surrender to the genius of a big cat sitting on it.

> *I have had many naps disturbed by surface embellishment. The remedy is to sit firmly in one place until all the ribbons and bows flatten."*
> —CLANCY

How Cats Invented Quilts & The Future of Cats and Quilting

"My oriental shorthair cat, Mylon, enjoys pulling needles out of my pincushion. My tabbycat Megan likes to help hold down fabric as I sew it. She also likes to check under the cutting board for invisible mice. Did I mention that they use my quilt frame as a hammock?"

— LISA LEFEVER,
MORAVIA, NEW YORK

How Cats Invented Quilts

We cats' playful interference with humans' craft projects through the centuries has resulted in many amazing advances in sewing, including the very invention of the quilt.

Medieval tailors were the first to stitch wool between layers of cloth. They did this in order to assemble heavy garments that they could wear to protect their arms as they struggled to remove their frolicking cats from their sewing baskets.

During the more enlightened Renaissance, these early quilted garments evolved into small tents. Needleworkers would band together in groups (later called quilting guilds). They would hide under the quilted tents in order to sew. As they did, their cats paced outside the tents, poking paws beneath to grope for loose thread or cotton snips to play with.

We cats eventually figured out how to crawl under the tents to smack pincushions across the floor and tussle with yarn. Sewers abandoned their tents—they tossed them on their beds. That's how quilts were born.

Humans soon found that they were unable to remove their quilted tents from their beds because their cats were sleeping on them. Since the humans' arms were unprotected (their quilted protective garments were also languishing on the beds), they did not care to endanger themselves by attempting to evict their cats. The cats remained on their beds. So did the quilts.

Eventually humans realized, as their cats had, that a quilt-covered bed was a pretty soft place to sleep. To this day, in many human households you will not see a quilt-covered bed without a cat sleeping upon it.

How Cats Improved Quilts

Many modern quilting techniques evolved in response to human quilters' need to assemble their quilts quickly before their cats ran into the room and pulled everything off the sewing machine.

Decorative hand-quilting patterns came into vogue in the 16th century when Italian quilters found themselves quilting around the behind of a large cat named Ferdinand.

Crazy quilts became the rage in 19th century America after a butter-scotch cat named Lulu rolled on an unsewn Baltimore album quilt, turning its tiny, fabric cut-outs of roses and leaves into a jigsaw puzzle that no one was able to piece back together again.

Many quilt patterns owe their existence to a cat eating a patch from the original pattern, and the quilter having to quickly improvise a solution with a scissors.

The Future of Cats and Quilting

As long as humans and cats need to snuggle into blankets in order to feel warm and secure, quilting will endure as an art as well as a passion for both species. It is our need to share our quilts with our friends, and by doing so share our warmth and spirit, which makes quilting the universal language of love that it is. As long as we cats make quilts, we will share them with our human friends, and hopefully vice versa.

And if our human friends don't share them with us—well, we'll sleep on them anyhow.

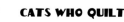
TEAR OUT CERTIFICATE:

Certificate of Membership in the League of Cat Quilters

TO ALL QUILTERS WHEREVER YE MAY BE and to all sewers, knitters, embroiderers, crocheters, tatters, needlepointers, bobbin-lace makers, weavers, and tole painters, GREETINGS!

Know ye that on this _____ day of _____ in the year _____

My cat _____ has passed all tests and inspections and been duly initiated into the LEAGUE OF CAT QUILTERS.

Be it known by whomever may be honored by his or her presence that membership in this League entitles one to Special Privileges including unlimited access to baskets containing pincushions and fabric snips, and the right to sleep undisturbed on any quilt in the house.

BE IT FURTHER KNOWN that as a member of the LEAGUE OF CAT QUILTERS he or she shall be revered in all places, particularly in sewing rooms and everywhere else where quilters congregate. In no instances shall a human chase this esteemed cat off a quilt, crying, "You're making a mess of things!"

FINALLY, all humans in the household will feel honored to have in their midst a GENUINE CAT QUILTER and will do all they can to further their cat's quilting career, including untangling thread from their cat's paws, fishing thimbles from his mouth, and unknotting fabric wound around his tail.

Clancy du Cotton
PAWDUCAH, KENTUCKY
SECRETARY

ABOUT THE AUTHOR

Judy Heim used to quilt until she realized that her cats do it better. She now spends most of her time encouraging her cats' development as quilters, as well as napping with them on their quilts. When she isn't ripping open bags of cat treats, she runs The Cat Quilt Web Site (**http://www.catswhoquilt.com**). She answers a lot of e-mail from cats. In her spare time, she writes books and magazine articles.

ABOUT THE ILLUSTRATOR

Irina Borisova is an award-winning cartoonist and animator whose animal characters have filled books, films, TV commercials, and theatres around the world for two decades. Many have been turned into ceramics and puppets. Her animated films have won many awards at European film festivals. She has her Art Gallery on the web (**http://www.mambor.com/Borisova/**). Originally from the Ukraine, she makes her home in Lenox, Massachusetts. She left her cat Cezar in the Ukraine. Although Clancy is modeled after Cezar, she used her husband Eugene as a stand-in model for many of the illustrations.